$T°$

# BELIEVE ME

## Lisa Sisneroz

$T$°
**THERA BOOKS**
Sacramento, California
SAY / SOMETHING

# Contents

Lefty . . . . . . . . . . . . . . . . . . . . . . . . . . . . . . . . . . . . . . . . . . . . . . 1

Compartmentalization . . . . . . . . . . . . . . . . . . . . . . . . . . . . . 3

A Roses Thorns . . . . . . . . . . . . . . . . . . . . . . . . . . . . . . . . . . . . . 5

Growing Pains . . . . . . . . . . . . . . . . . . . . . . . . . . . . . . . . . . . . . 9

Building from Broken Pieces . . . . . . . . . . . . . . . . . . . . . . 11

A Whole Half . . . . . . . . . . . . . . . . . . . . . . . . . . . . . . . . . . . . 14

Falling Leaves . . . . . . . . . . . . . . . . . . . . . . . . . . . . . . . . . . . . 16

Slits . . . . . . . . . . . . . . . . . . . . . . . . . . . . . . . . . . . . . . . . . . . . . . 18

Wasted . . . . . . . . . . . . . . . . . . . . . . . . . . . . . . . . . . . . . . . . . . . 21

The Tiny Thread . . . . . . . . . . . . . . . . . . . . . . . . . . . . . . . . . 23

Silence of the Storm . . . . . . . . . . . . . . . . . . . . . . . . . . . . . 26

No Content . . . . . . . . . . . . . . . . . . . . . . . . . . . . . . . . . . . . . . 30

Moonlight . . . . . . . . . . . . . . . . . . . . . . . . . . . . . . . . . . . . . . . 34

Inside Out . . . . . . . . . . . . . . . . . . . . . . . . . . . . . . . . . . . . . . . 37

Breathe . . . . . . . . . . . . . . . . . . . . . . . . . . . . . . . . . . . . . . . . . . 40

Manifesting . . . . . . . . . . . . . . . . . . . . . . . . . . . . . . . . . . . . . . 42

Dead Presidents
     (*Remix to *Dead Presidents* by Nas & Damian Marley) . 45

Poetry in Motion . . . . . . . . . . . . . . . . . . . . . . . . . . . . . . . . 48

Patience Remix
     (*Remix to *Patience* by Nas & Damian Marley) . . . . . . . 51

Natural Light . . . . . . . . . . . . . . . . . . . . . . . . . . . . . . . . . . . . 54

You . . . . . . . . . . . . . . . . . . . . . . . . . . . . . . . . . . . . . . . . . . . . . . 56

Just Visiting . . . . . . . . . . . . . . . . . . . . . . . . . . . . . . . . . . . . . 58

Because . . . . . . . . . . . . . . . . . . . . . . . . . . . . . . . . . . . . . . . . . . 62

Where the End Begins . . . . . . . . . . . . . . . . . . . . . . . . . . . . 65

Virtue Development . . . . . . . . . . . . . . . . . . . . . . . . . . . . . . 67

Loving Reflection . . . . . . . . . . . . . . . . . . . . . . . . . . . . . . . . 71

Endless . . . . . . . . . . . . . . . . . . . . . . . . . . . . . . . . . . . . . . . . . . 74

Acknowledgments . . . . . . . . . . . . . . . . . . . . . . . . . . . . . . . 77
Resources . . . . . . . . . . . . . . . . . . . . . . . . . . . . . . . . . . . . . . 79
About the Author . . . . . . . . . . . . . . . . . . . . . . . . . . . . . . . . 80

Dedicated to my baby love Juan.

You're my superhero.


The strength, thoughtfulness, determination, and compassion you effortlessly pour out into the world and the hearts that you encounter is just the beginning of what inspires me about you my lovey. Thank you because, without you, my heart wouldn't have known the full potential of what love and joy really are. Your heart is golden and built with purpose. Never forget the impact your presence makes. You are the strength that continues to inspire me and keep me trying another day. Thank you for proving to me that love is infinite. I hope you know how loved you are … But most importantly … Love yourself. I can't wait to see what other adventures you go on in life.


Being your mom is the best part of me.

I love you always son.

Never forget it.

for my peace within the storm, HIP HOP.

And too …

To those who've faced their own realities and who are still hurting
from trying to conceal their wounds.

For Anyone who's been unheard or broken.

For the visual creatives who bring words to life.

For artists.

For anyone debating if their heartbeat has a reason at all, it does.
That very anguish is what makes you shine, please stay.

For the voiceless, who learned too quickly how to hide their
sorrow with a smile.

For the forgotten.

For the victims of police brutality, as well as their loved ones.

For the misfits and goonz.

For the kids raised on the street embracing their environment
with pride for what strength builds.

For creatives who can't be who they are without their heart-work.

For those who were never found; the ones who never came back
home.

For the misery that reminded me why I continue to live.

## Lefty

How does one begin to fathom a thought process?
Then rearrange into a rhythmic pattern of words, metaphors,
    similes, and phrases just to be
oh just to be … complete?
Evaporating all the times in life is like
recollecting all the rhymes inside and I
know it's scary jumping into high tides but I
trust my wings spread 'em out and hope to fly

Painted story brushes dipped into the liquid from my eyes

As another soaks this page I ask myself wonder why

How's it taking me so long for the goals that I had planned?
Sure, we blame it on our struggles never had the upper hand.
But to see my left hand was right,
grip my pen there as I write.
Words encouraging
to find my purpose layin' deep inside
another page for the story one more chapter to unwind
perseverance pumping through my veins kiss my son goodnight
say I'm okay but not quite still see shadows in my mind
failed accomplishments keep taunting me

*come on bitch get it right!*
*if you're a tiger prove ya stripes*
*it's an ugly bumpy ride*

hands unsteady cannot find ways to overcome this climb
all these pills don't do shit
medication turned to lyrics
I inhale another beat
reflect
repeat and let 'em hear it—
it's just a tempo for the minds

another journey soon begins
travel through my tracks of time

# Compartmentalization

*Maybe if I*
start to let go of the pain I feel inside

*Maybe I try*
to let things blow over and
just whisper out my cries

*How can I fly*
with broken wings
feel the deepest of the nights
although strain has it's trouble
know within I will survive

*How can I cry*
without tears
doing enough too many years

Organized a box of hopeless thoughts
with tragedies and fears

Inside my mind, hid that time ...
only I see what's inside.

Now the chapters building up
showing pages of my life

Overflowing had me going, can I shove it back inside?

*Oh what a mess!*
I do confess, know I shouldn't try to hide
from my emotions left unspoken out of sight N out of mind

What's the problem, was it me?
Something that I didn't see?
Lesson that I had to learn?

Guess my life had to turn,
 no more cutting,
 no more burns
Yearning for a new escape … but scars won't set me free so I
    turn another page

Maybe if I let myself cry
Maybe I'll see beauty beneath
Maybe if I hold myself tight

maybe I'll be stronger and free

Foggy daze embraces truth … reflect on older days

Broken pieces molded me,
 cannot flee can't fade away

So I greet them day to day …

*What's up anxiety, depression*
*thought I seen ya round the way … don't ya ever need a break?*

*Are ya tryna test my rage?*
*Don't know how much I can take*
*Never fold I find a way, but you been here since second grade*

See piles of my pain, when's it ever gonna change?
no more hiding what I'm fighting
now I write another page.

# A Roses Thorns

3 percent of girls were age ten or younger the time of their first
   rape
44 percent of rapes with penetration occur before the age of
   eighteen
The use of secrecy, blame, and threats are used to maintain
   control
No longer will they maintain a hold

Questions left unanswered linger through my mind
Years of wondering
still behind

Tuck in corners of the bed so they're incapable to find
Will my fear get the best of me? Can I put up a fight?

*Eyes shut tight.*

Begin the terror of night.

Heart screams for help, voice can't get the words right
Am I the first for you?
Will I be the last?
And how long will this horror last?
Shattered past of my youth, innocence no longer true

Holds my throat as he whispers … if you tell no-one will care

Hands rip every part of me, reveal the ugly truth

inside a lost child
worthless
broken
hushed and confused

enduring pain not just from you

cuz after him

there were many more too

realize then it's sink or swim
another bed I lay on
awaiting escape
soon enough another nightmare
approached to seal my fate

Close your eyes
as we run throughout time.
No rose can bloom without it's thorns
Soon enough you'll be alright
Hear the stories of a child's broken dream
Close your eyes, leave your mind
try to imagine what I mean

Close your eyes as we run throughout time.
Pushing vivid memories to the back of my mind
Rewind back in time
shall I dare press play?
They told me I would heal but I never been the same

Hear stories on the news never thinking it'd be you
Tried to tell my story once, cops said there's nothing to pursue

Cops saying: Did he do it … are you sure … did you even get
    proof?

Childlike mentality flew straight out the roof

Decided to endure it, so my friends won't go through it
Thought, if I took this burden all to myself, then he wouldn't
    dare try to lay his hands on
someone else

Like a book on a shelf I was a chapter left inside
Screaming in my head, no one to hear the fight

As I wake to daylight, I see a new me

Forgot the young, loving, girl I used to be
Below the belt hands they sneak tearing every part of me

Still it's not enough for your family to see
leave the side of the innocent

The Guilty set free

One story of plenty
Silenced voices speak to see

Felt like it's my fault for not saying more

But how can someone not hear what's going on behind the
    doors
Silently beg *no more* as he enters the room
Coming closer
hear the steps
a life forever doomed

As he sneaks in, I try to hide underneath
As I curl on the edge, I start to cry
As my clothes come off, I'm here frozen in time
My new cycle begins, will I ever escape?

Chasing night and day, now I'm finding my new way

Close your eyes as we run throughout time
No rose can bloom without it's thorns
Soon enough you'll be alright
Hear the stories of a child's broken dream
Close your eyes, leave your mind
try to imagine what I mean

Close your eyes as we run throughout time.
Pushing vivid memories to the back of my mind
Rewind back in time shall I dare press play?
They told me I would heal but I never been the same

# Growing Pains

Tell me if this pain is worth it now that I've said it out loud?

Are you proud of this child
or the one who used to be?

Can you still see me?

Who I am inside
and all that lies beneath

Now do you see my fears?

or wish
I'd rather not speak?

Do you think you'd hesitate if I woke you that night?

Would you still insist to fight if it were someone you loved?

Your own against one another ...

Tell me ... who would get the hug?

exactly.

Add *that* to more reasons,
right under the rug.

I knew the mess it'd make if brought above.

maybe sometimes when I cuss
and say you could've done more

I forget about the times
you fell to the floor

praying for an answer
from one you can't see

Enraged yet in lined,
yet still protected your seed.

weakened knees tremble as excuses fade into air.

Glaring over us
like a crow to its prey

hollow

*knowing* this wouldn't be his last day.

*Please keep trying … don't let them leave …*

*What's it gonna take for them to believe?*

I know she saw us cuz he made me look too.

This is why my reflection to this day feels untrue.

Sirens slowly disperse one after one.

… confused
broken
internally bruised

Goodbye innocence.
while it lasted, it was fun.

# Building from Broken Pieces

Tears shed while you grabbed and groped.
When you told me I was beautiful, I was sick to my throat.
Silent screams left me frozen, unable to see, unable to realize
    what would be left of me.
Hands sharp as glass shattering away
what little remains of my smile
taking the innocence that was left of a child

*was I the first? will I be the last*
just *how fucking long* will this horror last?

enduring pain but not only from you
because after him
there were many more too
always seems to be the ones closest to

when you bought me that baseball glove
was it for me or your guilt
did you ever realize the monster you'd built
afraid to love
afraid to see
afraid to listen, speak, think
to grow
to try to feel alive

Do you know how it is
to not even want to look in your own eyes?

Reflections were empty before I knew it.
My life was meaningless to the point I felt determined to prove
    it.
Turned to cutting and running away from my mind.

Baggy clothes, ratted hair, afraid to catch someone's unwanted
    eye.

Countless years, *still* fucking wondering why

Spoke my story before but only one part.
every occurrence afterwards
I simply didn't have enough heart

to speak when I'm afraid
cuz look what it cost.

Was it worth my life?　　　　Is it worth it now?
Now that he's facing the same charges against his own child?

then it matters　but not for me
although I'm glad she can finally be free

somehow for years I knew she was suffering beside me
through the mess I hope she can rebuild
what's left of her
and I'm sorry for saying no to testifying with you
I simply didn't hold the courage to be as brave as you
I remember what my family said
once I let out the truth
"He didn't even put it all the way in, so why does it count?"

No ...

　　　　no ...

　　　　　　no ...

　　　　　　　　　　you'll never know the amount
amount of terror from sleepless nights
different men sneaking into my beds
wherever I went no home was an escape
soon enough there's a new one
creeps in to seal my fate
as he creaks opens the door ... I try to scream
as he walks over ... I curl on the edge and try to hide

as he gets in bed … I start to cry
as my clothes come off … I'm here again
frozen in time still wondering why

fast forward fifteen years
I'll tell you what's next
time turned those tears into moments held to reflect
Time spent wondering why
why you say not to speak of it if it's okay?
why do you sneak, when supposedly it's a game to play
why choose me now
why again and again?

I began immune to this once
time sealed my fate
Now, time of horror is done
Now, time to wait

wait to rebuild
wait to heal
a way to truly express how I feel
but not here
not now
that's up to me to figure out for myself

# A Whole Half

Sometimes I feel like a waste of a woman.
Maybe that's too forward
Maybe half of one or less than
I don't want to put myself down too much
but i would like to absorb every
descriptive
vivid
even negative thought so I don't let them pass by.

Every feeling is precious
so I'll try

To let myself creep in slowly
to get a grip
before I slip
into puddles with frantic preparation
to withstand the pressure
applied by words
that surround this pool of emotions
I'm about to dive into

I'm a woman you can hardly touch.
I hate it about myself
that I feel I can't give my partner enough.

I'm seductive in ways I don't attempt.
If I do, I can't fully please, if I don't
well fuck just I'm a tease!

You see *these* ... are the thoughts
I mean,
Am I woman enough for me?

Am I proud enough to know it's not my role
to provide all the fantasies of societies dreams

To the world,
I am incomplete
cuz I've bared only one child.

No siblings
No needs met
And no holding back when they say:
"C'mon, you were so young, just try again …
He needs someone to play with
to laugh and share silly jokes."

Guilt trip me with that shit as if I don't already know.
Countless doctor visits ended with little hope
is what they don't see.

*"Not likely a possibility."*

Try that shit for a taste.

Paired with a side of … *maybe in the future,
but your ovaries aren't that great.*

All I ask is that you consider thinking twice before asking
    family members, friends, and colleagues when they plan to
    have a kid.

or how much longer till there's more.

Cuz you've got no damn clue
the pain that heart has already endured.

# Falling Leaves

I pace around quickly so you won't catch a glimpse
hiding silence with laughter

Forced smile ... Clutched fists.

Hello misery, I knew you'd be back again.

Is it okay to pretend if no one else knows?
If I'm lucky, maybe next time I'll get to keep on my clothes.

if I act like I'm away it's not as bad as it seems.

Thinking that line back once again

*Imagine yourself sitting in the tallest tree*
*where no one can touch you or grab as they please.*

Only leaves decide when it's time to fall.

Weakened branches grew restless
holding more than they can take

ironic though human
I too carried that weight

subtle crack to be heard
breath thrown to the floor

heart sank to the knees
as he walked towards my door

color range change ...
dries up from its days

brittle and crisp

before it crumbles away

drifting with the wind
light as can be
scattered pieces float towards every which way

No direction is taken
they go as they please                              oh how I
    wish I can be as free as the leaves.

# Slits

This may be a familiar road traveled
or one too far to grip
descriptions won't define the depth of how far in you might slip
back to the basics with a mindful twist

an abundance of stories with no-one to hear

Chocking up on her words
swallow the rage to try to clear it

Tried in every way not to be less than perfect
still she serves a purpose
Based by the family tree
not many leaves are attached but her love she can still see

Although it's a glimpse
nothing left unless
family wishes to grow and build

Still it's not on them to blame cuz who went first?
was it the mother or the daughter who inflicted this curse?
or was it really her fault cuz her grandmother didn't know the
        worth
of a child
of a dream
of a heart incomplete
of a rite of passage never crossed
so she daydreams in her sleep
cuz the mind never closes
she never really gets peace
Although she's tried to drank to blackout many times

Attempts to put the nightmares to sleep

till a night she decides it may not be as bad as she thinks

in the blink of an eye the slit is now there
blood dripping down her thighs
silent screams
leaking everywhere

*this will be the last time*

telling herself one more soothing lie
quietly packs her tools away as she rests her head to fly
In that moment pain seemed real
Finally she's in control of when it starts and when it stops
relief somehow as blood stains dry
meaning she made it thru once more

Hope to find an escape but shit there's that banging on the door

if you don't get out here and clean this shit up
Ima come back for more

*I'll be there in a minute*

Falls crying to the floor
Dirty tiles and towels now soaked with her pain
tiny glimpse of hope but inside she knows she'll never change

destined to be broken

Cleans the blood off the sink
Resin seeps down to the pipe lines settling down into the core

Screaming *stop it! please no more! I'm sorry i'll be strong!*

But she never listens to herself
Just another trait to add to the list of why she fuckin hates
        herself
Cuz she's been told she's wrong all along

This was not meant to be a song
it's meant to be a way
to present soft spoken voices a lighter time of day
Maybe they can use this pain from my past and rebuild self-love
true love that will last

Minds moving too fast
we're running out of hope
Not enough time left in the world to put in the effort to cope
Cuz that means you'd have to listen instead of trying to speak
Hear to understand
Speak to reveal
Learn to move on right past these ordeals
A mind unhealed can be a powerful thing
Once it begins to see it's worth
it can accomplish many things
But we're still here

I'm in stage one

Finally realizing what I am and who I've become
Vigorous.
Beautiful.
And cultivated in grace …
A wandering soul who now knows her place

# Wasted

You're like a zombie with its mind in a trance

I look past the picked scabs
all across your face
cuz every time you relapsed
feels I'm the one who made the mistake

what's the fate of one's purpose
when the soul's no longer there?

popping up at different hours
bangs on doors as I prepare

Scared to see your conditions worsen
dilated blank stare
once upon a time it was my loved one in there
now the body's incomplete
the smoke takes shape of your memories
before vanishing into air
yet wildly with no form
leaving its trail of scorned love and families torn

Tell me ...
When did the voices in your head become louder than the
    truth?

play along for a moment as if we can't tell you're using
I pretend that we're content
as if drugs you're not abusing

what hurts the most
is you don't even see
the struggles we deal with seem to go unheard
whether its hiding behind your fears
or not fully projecting words

methamphetamine
lenos
P.C.P
fucking oblivious needs

my tears relapse as you reply

"No see you don't understand it's the drug that needs me! …
it needs my hand to hold the lighter
to flicker its flame
extra one to hold the pipe
ensuring to liquify its content properly as it bubbles just right
similar to teamwork ya see?!"

evaporating fumes leave lifelong stains

"it needs the tight grip from my lips
so the access smoke won't fade astray
every last hit counts
with the amount I've got left …"

oh yeah          I say
you're four hours sober
*now* I see why you were so stressed

# The Tiny Thread

When I look at you
I see me

I don't mean our facial features that match
although we're very similar on that too
I mean the hurt soul inside that never got the love it desired
When you call me crying because they won't accept you
after all you've done
I hear my screams I muffled in the pillow every night
after I tried to prove to you throughout the years that you don't
    need their love

you've got mine

Still that was never enough nor will it be
When I give you advice how to move on from them
I realize I need to take listen to it as well
And although I have been doing so lately
the heart is not rebuilt overnight

I tell you
    Love them from afar

stop expecting them to change

Don't be hopeful for them to see your pain and you won't be
    hurt

Shit I need to listen to my own words
Why is it so hard?
Is this what I deserve?
Maybe I'm a fucked-up person for telling you in the manner I
    just did
but I was just a kid
More mature than any adult had to be

Mind focused on bills, errands, drug use, household mainte-
nance, healthcare,
sexual abuse escape plans
containing broken pieces of a family
A family that you could have removed me from
situations you could have prevented
feelings and family secrets that should have been revealed
scars that together we could have healed
I was a child then
but not anymore
The advice I give
I know it's effective cuz I've been doing it with you
As well as the remaining people in my life who proved their
love untrue
I know it works cuz when I hear you cry about the same things
I've experienced for so long
it doesn't affect me as much
Not AS much … Not anymore

Yes

I get sad and pissed off how you speak every feeling of mine so
vividly
It's like you see me but you don't
Am I a daughter or a ghost?
You haven't realized you're still doing the same to me
You don't comprehend how it hurts to hear
as you weep how you'll never be enough for who you adore

My love always felt invisible in your eyes

Unheard and unbothered
So why do I try?
I repeat to myself

just shut up and take your own advice

Yet that tiny thread of hope I still hold in my hand cuz my

dumbass is still hopeful
Imagining one day
you'll understand

# Silence of the Storm

Waking up to pounding and screams at the door

"come quick your mom is passed out on the bathroom floor
something wrong but I don't know"

not the first lie he told

ran so fast just to find
her mother's body cold

Foam dripping out her mouth, slow pulse, muttered words
flash back every memory even ones that hurt.
Small bucket for the trash overflowed with her blood
sight no eyes should ever have to see of someone they love.
Soaked towels scatter cross the floor
screams for help

"c'mon brother wake up sister!"

"let's carry mom out"

"start the car get it ready!"

they beg to her man

"no she'll make my car a mess,
just call an ambulance …"

phone seemed so far
brother picks her up
carries mom to the couch saying, "please don't give up!"

Everything went mute.

Paramedics rush through

Older sister calms her nephew quietly in the next room.
Reflection brother's eyes never seemed so doomed
kissed her forehead jumps in ambulance and slams the door.
Chased after it and peeks into the window once more.

This day was supposed to be good                    her
    very first job.

Second day panning pizzas
washing dishes as she sobs.
Sitting on her lunch break when she gets the call.
"Sorry princess, Mom's in surgery it's looking pretty bad … You
    should head over here after,
she's got a slim chance."

Her intestines were turning
the devil played his dance.
Rotting her bodily organs killing everyone she's got …

Kids handle more bills. Forced to stay in that spot.
Contribute seven bucks an hour hope to fill the melting pot.
Manager says, "go now! cuz families all you got!"
Bus never came
running home out of breath
elevator rises to ICU
she takes the first step.

Walking thru the hallways
she now gets the talk …

"Don't be scared when you see her          mentally try to
    prepare.
What you remember of momma is no longer there."

Tubes and bags now plug her into her new life.
Surgeons say it was tough but she put up a fight.
Removed are her dead intestines less than a foot left.

*Monitoring her now then well run some more tests.*

Days go by a silent house no longer a home.
Siblings curled in mom's bed never felt so alone.

Waking up to more screams to realize it's her own

"I miss mommy," she cries
"when she gonna come home?"

Time passes ...

College seems to drain her
freshmen at the time
try to focus on a lecture holding tears in her eyes.

Holds her veins
mom's blood still on her sweater
not a stain but a change                                    a scar
    forever.

Light rail town to town trying to make her proud.
Never had the strength to do it so she can't just drop out

Ring ring* are you there?

More bad news:

"Take a seat we need to speak, I'll be over soon.
See baby the thing is ... after another surgery,
Mom slipped into a coma, please be strong.
Doctors say she can't hear us, but we can still sing her songs."

And ...

"Make some calls to your family ... Think they should be here
    too
say your goodbyes while you can

it's not likely she'll pull through."

looks to brother squeezed his hand
troubled
what to do?
There's no family to call who does he think we are?
It's always been us and just three of my friends …
Whose love turned to trust
while blood ones played pretend

Once the word gets out were not outcasts anymore.
Old family sweeps in lining up at the door.
Fights with every fucking member who tried to step in.
They don't deserve to be here just to leave her again.
Hearing her in pain for years after they all shut her out.
Leaving her in tears with two kids left to her name
who had to figure life out.
Gone so long and now ya changed?
Audacity of people                               guess we'll never be
        the same.
Snapping pictures of y'all together hashtag ya fucking tears
posting:

*"pray 4 my family please, were all in fear"*

get that shit up out her face
good thing security is here

# No Content

You may think by the title of this, there's nothing really to hear
but if you pay attention
recall details from before
you'll see encrypted messages speak loud and clear

*Is it all she's good for?*

Guess she'll never know
Caregiver for her mother remember dreams that didn't grow
Hard times a low blow
no emotion left to show
paving what she thought was an example seems so long ago
Failed attempts fall ... Await for her rise

Flooded by the blossoms
falling from the sky

cherry colored pink soars across the skyline

pain runs deep
still she's stays by her side
Siblings tend to leave
depart once more ... Slowly making their way one by one out
    the door

The one who stays ... The one who was last
Broken hearted daughter
hope for change shattered glass

Not the right time or never focused frame
Crazy as it seems
mental beating take the pain
Maybe this way she'd see how much she cares
never seen the picture heart leaks everywhere
Left to clean the mess another night and day

Cries in bed as she lays

raining tears stain her face

Mother's love can erase but look at the time

been hurting here for years everyone say she's fine

Chase after a heart
she's loved a lifetime
It was never enough
trips late to the store ...

"if you don't get up get my meds, you'll be sorry for sure!"

*yes mom I'm comin'*        *please don't be upset*

"grab food while you're there and this time don't forget!"

add it to the list and mark it down with a check

Can't replace what's empty
love never true.

Blurry nights aren't as scary if you squint your eyes.
Sunrise became a factor
fear of her mind meant another day of tears
she'd have to hide.

Night fall approaches
finally she can shine.

Notebooks full of stories
chapters of her mind.
Pages soaked with tears of hope.
Words that never found the time.
Can't speak of these things
even if she tried.

still won't justify the hurt        not even a word
tuck emotions back in
fuck it all its no worth

Back to work another long day
she tucks her son
into bed then they pray his joy helps her overcome

Says we'll be alright
inside those words she fights

Try to raise a man above hope she's doing it right.

Mirror has no reflection
what she really wished to see
damaged goods valued junk all she seemed to be

Living in a daze
she starts to learn
packs her bags days before eighteen no plan to return.

*Gotta love myself mom, so my son I can show … environment for the
heart must be watered to grow. So although I truly love you I've
got to go*

Puts the past behind
she's free at last.

Moving on to renting rooms with little to no cash
Promised her son the world cuz he gave her life back
Every ounce of love she ever wanted before from a sweet baby
boy
there's nothing more pure.
Now the hearts complete
search is over
see the world Juanito
strong as a soldier

Brave young man
She already sees.
Proud to stand by his side
his love is all she needs.

Take my hand
let's go
you lead the way

Mommy's always behind you
footsteps never fade.
Thank you for listening to all of my tears
while never once turned away
wish I can take back those years

I remember how hard to see tears on grandma's face
emotionally scarred had to learn a different way

Hopefully, I can be the one to break the chain
so you won't have to fight love just cuz you're feeling pain.

Take it all and use it
it'll help you move on

I love you always son.

Yours truly,                                   your mom

# Moonlight

Gazing at the stars with this part on repeat
Moon may not produce it's light but it's shining on me

Would revealing all my worries really take away the pain?
Don't like falling asleep cuz it brings me back again to the
    memories of hopelessness
sitting in a mess

Stronger I confess but that don't mean I get my rest

Conflicted in decisions as I try to break the chains
See a light beyond the distance
but a shadow on my face try to uncover
How
to challenge my fate
step back for a moment then adjust my happy face

This heart bears more weight than I can take on my chest
Take a pause for a moment cuz I can't feel my breath

Cuz when I'm healing
feel I'm breaking different parts of my soul
cuz those shattered pieces once were
what was making me whole

Take control of my emotions with the stroke of a pen
creating new realities as I inhale notes within

who would've been there for me if I can't write down these
    words?

cannot pour from empty cups so take the love you deserve

To first begin your healing can't pretend you're not hurt

Blood and tears in this verse
measurements of it's worth
So even if it gets no play
know I threw with a curve
if your intentions aren't genuine don't step to the plate
Smiling faces telling lies always cautions for snakes
helping hands hiding knives without leavin' a single trace
Temptations and O'Jays coulda taught you these things
you too distracted by the mess and not the lesson it brings

I exist
for the willingness to nurture my seed
Standing guard when under pressure
Push him to open wings
He's a being of grace magnified by the sun
Simply blessed within his presence
baby steps to a run
Baby boy you have come further than I can dream
Promise I will carry you like trees for the leaves
Certain moments you may fall
feeling short and in doubt
Just remember mommy's words                    you can
     figure it out

See the moonlight
the moonlight is hazy
but the moonlight
the moonlight it gave me

Chance to start another chapter daily
it's amazing
how it saved me

Back against the wall feel my face on the ground

Voices echoing around me
yet I can't hear a sound

except the beat as it pounds

Toss a line to escape
suddenly I feel my body lifting up in a wave
No more fighting my brain
now we dancing in sync
So prepare for the worst                               it's not as
        bad as you think

But still hope for the best
know it's hard when you're stressed
Make a plan see it through and be aware of your steps

Those tears become the water that refreshes your roots
Yet can also be the droplets coming crashing through your roof
Take a loss with stories earned
not simply just regrets
poetic harmony saved me when I had nothing left
can't take anything back once you visit with death

Turning pain into a promise
never settle for less
Reflecting on different days found a way to build hope
with the lines upon this page when I feel I cannot go on …

# Inside Out

The day you ripped that card you ripped a piece of my heart.
Only one I had left from back from the start.

When I was too young to understand
 after effects of love

What happens when you give your all to someone who does
not see the truth of your actions and words …

Try to twist it, to flip it, to inflict the hurt.

But here I go again, you screaming thru the phone.
Telling me that I'm evil cuz I refuse to visit your home.

Mom, it's hard to stay away. Harder to keep close, your abuse
    drives me astray.
Every time I'm with you I still get hurt.
It's my fault in the end maybe it's what I deserve.

Don't understand your words.
When you speak, I can't hear
cuz all I can see are the reflections of my tears.

Am I broken? Am I good? Will I ever be enough?
Guess you didn't want my love
guess it just didn't add up.

As I chase after your heart, you're running toward theirs.

Pick up the pieces, fall apart, no hesitation anywhere.
When they left you for the others, remember who was there

Wouldn't even call you mother but you still fucking cared

Maybe…

One day I can make you proud.

But for now every day, I gotta say it to myself.
Failed attempts to build with the only one I loved.

Two hearts incomplete
many reasons to cry ...
The irony is, I heard it from inside
your own body but you still won't attempt to hear mine ...

Repetitive range of emotions but you say that we're fine

"they're your family just forgive them"

heard it too many times

At a young age I thought, and then I had a plan:

*If i clean up the house and cook for her man,
she'll pay attention to me and realize who I am.*

Behaved myself in church dripping with sweaty hands
sitting beside my misuser she was put on a stand
don't ask me why cuz I still can't comprehend

Mom I'm sorry
i still love you but I'm tired of this pain
when I'm gone
please don't wonder or ask why I changed

I went to find peace for my heart to live in.
Hold our memories of hope as my pain seeps in ...

So when they start to reject you and call you out your name,
don't say I never loved you cuz my love never changed.

I love you ... I hate you

I hate what we've become.

I'm still here for you mom but look at all you've done.

Tell the family all our secrets that'll never be done. Blaming me
  to put me down only helps me overcome.

Mom,
please don't make me open up all the truth we went through cuz
  somehow there's still love.

Somehow I still trust ...
Somehow I still cope ...

Our love is a lost cause,
Mom I've lost hope.

I love you forever mom.
I hope you still love me after hearing this.

But what I've learned from a lifetime of loving you is that I
  need to love me.
Even if it means distancing myself from who I love the most ...

I'm sorry I couldn't fix us.
Hope we can still love somehow ... You'll always be my
  definition of hope.
Love always,

the last one

# Breathe

*Breathe momma!*

cuz I can't hear ya tone

I said

*breathe momma! please don't leave me alone!*

Feel her pulse slowing down with every second I break
foam fizzing out the mouth
could she ever be the same?

skin is colder than the winter when we had no clothes

why's he screaming in my face
needs to get the damn phone

running into my room tryna wake up the fam
can't believe she put all trust in that twisted man
was it part of his plan        guess the world will never
    know
cuz he didn't even rush
    mothafucka tip toed

boasting on later how he saved her life.
Messed up part was that she took his side

Staring into the eyes of who gave me birth
felt my heart cry then but she didn't hear a word

Yearned for a love that never survived
it never existed
no matter how I tried

Fighting Jedi mind tricks as I'm looking at you

said I'm tired of this pattern you keep putting me through
I kept going back
damn I'm smarter than that!

What will it take to see the fact that this lesson is long

Teach myself how to heal whilst writing this song
bouncing back on the rhythms that I have to take

Gave the lyrics time to speak as I lay here awake
underneath my pillow lies the tears

they're fading away

No more pieces to break
letting go of your stress.

As much as I still love you
my heart needs it's rest
I confess it's never easy when you're calling my line
Ring, ring, quick decision …

Should I answer this time?

True that love makes you blind

truly makes me think.

How in hell I gave my all to an imperfect being
type of things really sting when it's close to home

rather live by myself than wit you all alone

# Manifesting

I'm manifesting my strength.
Overcoming fears.

Doubted my abilities for one too many years

Once the ground starts to quake, I know what to do.

Hell and back was insane
but it helped me to improve ooh ... who am I, to say that it's
    done?

Beginning of the book,

you're only seeing page one

What rolls around in chapter two, is not for me and you

Couple things that I keep to myself..
 it's my view.

No offense to your mind, just my heart's been in a bind

Accepting my truth
but you can't read between the lines.

Time has its chances,
what is it for?

Will you learn from mistakes? Or go back for some more?

Take it as a lesson
All who abandoned me, I see it as a blessing

I'm not stressed
I'm impressed,

that I still cared … and how I kept holding on,

when I knew it wasn't fair,
man my love, it stayed strong

Gave endless affection
genuine and pure.

But life is too short to keep banging on their doors

Or …

maybe *this time* I'd finally be heard …

But I'm past that stage now.
My heart you don't deserve.

All ya got left of me is everlasting words.
Pitching game with a curve

analyze what you heard.

An elegant frame filled with powerful hurt.
Not merely the surface, it dwells deep inside.

Beauty, pain, and passion
equally intertwined.

The depths of my mind are crafted with age.
Sometimes it builds me up
it can also be a cage
filled with rage and emotion,
heart racing convulsions inspired I'm hoping

grapple thoughts as I'm chocking.

hands begin to tremble

I need an instrumental to get a grip on the shit
overflowing my mental … It's overflowing my mental

# Dead Presidents
### (Remix to *Dead Presidents* by Nas & Damian Marley)

See it's hard when you're coming from pain,
inflicted down to your roots forever holding rusted chains.

As I carry on this weight thinking how I can make a change
instantly I catch a glimpse of a future lost in its ways

Too many innocent lives enduring pain
backs up against the wall guns drawn it's insane.
cuz they ain't even a teen, getting slammed to the ground
no longer can we scream

Standing up for your rights
can get you arrested for making a scene,
with no sleep tonight.

As I close my eyes await for better days think back …
I ask the dead presidents:
*what's the purpose of your last act?*
Give us hope cuz we don't have that.

Honestly, it's hard when you can't breathe.
Just the sight of their lights brings resurfaced memories.
Too many scenes, too many scars, too many times our families
thrown up against the cop's car      hands up don't shoot please!
We got dreams and kids too can't you see?!
Not as different as it seems
serve and protect by *any means*
What's your reasoning to watch him die before your eyes
you want my symphony
nowhere in sight
Still our voices and protests won't make it on t.v.
blinded and misguided hopes of perfect reality
What's the cause, what's the cure, whatever can it be
we're only asking simple questions thinking logically.

Land of endless opportunities somehow we're not free.
Kids planning funerals while the shooters on paid leave
Weapon at hand was the position of power.

Reoccurring memories, every minute every hour
cries for help throughout the walls
we'll never hear the sound

Locked eye contact
        as his breathing slowed down ...

If it were your son,
 would you have done something else?

See, that's the thing you can't explain, words can't describe that
        change

Emotions roam
Now his kids will spend Father's day alone

Silenced voices rise to speak
seems we'll never make a change

polished lies,
apologies ...        that don't justify the pain,

our lives will never be the same.

No Justice No Peace
candles lit for the deceased

Tell me not to point the finger ...        as far as I can see,

He never had the right to determine what
their lives were meant to be

So how the fuck are we free?

Watch the swiftness of a snake
perpetrators freed the gates
As the family grieves to fill the void what that legend once
        made

Can't expect silence once you've shaken up a crowd
Defend the lives of many don't choose who goes without.

Human rights in reality is shaken and brewed

Only life they show,
 is taken out of context in the news …

Yet play family videos and barbecues
if the uniform is pressed
in shiny black and blue

# Poetry in Motion

To you it's just a story, to us it's a life.
Poetry in motion
day one full of strive
conflicted with hurt
block out memories inside
never really knew the worth
as I buried down the past
ask myself if I'm cursed
tears came rushing back
shove it down with all I've got
cuz I ain't going back

severity of the issues

Reflect,
see impact

of a life unsheltered
never faced a concern

*is it my fault?*

or was just it my turn?

to see the ugliness
the truth
will force you to learn

descriptive
my intentions
were to bring a brighter light

those inflicted by the shadows
bringing terror to their nights

dwelling in your sorrows
gats on the ground
let your voice make the sound
empty bullets soar the town

missed the target
now a kid
is slain on the ground

dreams come to a hold
mother's nightmare watched
as the body turns cold
almost had the month's rent
to finally leave town
but another day spent
gone too fast
she never saw it
never had a chance

youth tryna prove themselves
hopes of early advance

only proves that were lost
proves that were scared

only proves that were broken

in need of repair
invisible scars start to bleed
seeping everywhere
one of many stories, cease to an end
it's more than a life
it's a cycle that were in
soak it
absorb it
reflect your pain within
cuz without that horror

light would never shine the same
call it rhythm and rhymes
a way to slow down time
grasping onto the day dreams
that's impossible to find
hope that I can do that
if I react in time

bookmark pages of the heart
chapters of the mind

highlight my insights
a better place to find
for now I'll be here
writing what's inside
as I listen to the soft breeze
of the leaves
flying by …

listen to the soft breeze of leaves flying by

# Patience Remix
### (*Patience* by Nas & Damian Marley)

Distant memories of chasing clouds,
embasking time …

Lyrically beautiful
embrace in full
the message of her rhymes

We're all anxious for the wealth, won't put in effort or the time
    …

Punching in and out ain't easy cooperate world or on the side

To seal your fate, the streets awaits.
Deadly cycle soon begins …
Reaching for a better future your whole life now does depend

No pretend
moderate to deviate
protect your soul …

Never know the fears unleashed once harming thoughts just
    take control

Mind is sharper than a blade
 still she's lost up in the ways …
unbroken          what to do?

Prevails

still submerging in her ways—

*Instantly she's sinking in*
lungs are closing deep within,
thoughts of pressure building up …          feeling depression

creeping in

The intention of ambition

Now she's diving right back in,     realization I can do it
see me grinnin tryna win

Now I see what was beneath
new improved version of me

Leaving your fears unresolved
won't make it better
can't you see
 it just takes patience

Is there nothing left to do?
Cooperation                          with their greed.

Starving families in the streets
broken economy it seems

Giving away money for game shows
and lotto's every week
Tell me where the funds are from, deceptions sometimes hard
     to see

It has now become the ugly truth
 of our new normality

Blinded by the packs of wolves
 hiding under clothes of sheep …

Unrevealed remedies they've achieved from the past..

Patience is a virtue
getting lost in the schemes will not last

Diligence will slowly build you,

lose focus it might kill you

Presence of mind,
    pen and paper ...

Inspiration, yes I'll take it

Feel the truth
as it's soaking in, fuel pumping through your veins
Blurred vision finally clears back up
realize it's time to change

Money makes the world go round ...
        can also tear that shit right down.

Watch the company you keep

Mischievous, slithering on the ground,
seek to play games in your life

Will you fall or will you rise?

Take opportunities and flip it, prove you can be a light
    just takes patience

# Natural Light

Watching you open up the curtains beside me
your arms stretch above my head towards the top of the window

as you tie the securing knot that opens them
I see the whole room brighten up

what was once covered in darkness is now
visible to the naked eye

crumpled up snot filled tissues surround me
refills resting right underneath my hands

cuz we both know at the rate my tears
have been flowing lately

I was going to reach for more at any moment
but not this one.

At this moment there is light beaming upon me
both literally and hypothetically

the moment you opened the curtains
you looked down to me and smiled

smiled as if you didn't even mean to
not to make me happy cuz I was down

or to get one
in return

but as if it were just natural reaction
when you catch a quick glimpse of me you smile.

After that I thought to myself
in the upmost lovingly cheesiest way possible

That man reaching above me
is love.

And let me just add this specific love
is far brighter than the rays of sunshine he let in that afternoon

Seconds later I chuckled at the irony
of seeing the light of my life
bringing light into my life.
Unknowingly from this view

as if it were second nature
I reacted with a simple smile

just like him moments before
I realized why he still smiled so sweetly as he seen me sitting in
    my darkness

Which is that I too am his light
I too give him love when he hides in his shadows

Just as he sits beside me in mine until
I'm ready to be seen

So thank you handsome
for sharing your light with me

# You

I hate when I can't fix shit and I know that don't sound right

See my problems are, these thoughts will keep me wide awake
   at night

Why should I fight with a past that is no longer there?

Evaluating lessons learned so I can be better prepared

Cuz I'm scared and I'll admit it
And I've said it once before

Every time I saw my son walking out the front door

I knew this life wouldn't, always quite be the breeze
but I built him with endurance, perseverance in his being
cuz I know one day he'll have to walk that road without me

hopefully in moments of that stress he remembers to breathe

These types of moments you can never take back
and you can cry baby love

I'm proud of you for that

You can do it Baby Love
go and spread your wings to fly

Forget about the ground beneath you
Jump and make it to the sky

I believe

if you try
you can conquer it all

Accept your battles

Keep your head high and always
stand tall

## Just Visiting

I realize where I am as the familiar sense
of beautiful rage overflows out of me

Here with you again

next to you always feels so far from myself

You got me once more

pacing circles around the faded desires of when I *wished* we'd
    have this talk

dreamed of you confessing the hurt inflicted

I knew you knew
but it's okay

because it became possible to me

to simply visit the *idea* of us and what we *would* be
*if* we ever *could*

as if your love were displayed in this museum of my mind

Dwelling on this piece

I absorb
what patience and focus was needed to create it

the courage needed to display this version of yourself

Teardrops stained the corners of that page in your life
causing the smallest wrinkles only seen by the one who lost
    them

Yes      it's still worthy of admiration and deserving of love

"Damaged hearts are still beautiful."

Unknowingly you taught me this

I'm a frequent visitor of this specific gallery
because every year more art is
added            not exchanged

even the frame can hardly keep holding onto this heavy piece of
        heart
*I will carry it for you*

So here I am again.

Gazing at your love

your patience
still in awe

just as much as when I was a kid

*I will love you more*

I reach to touch
but fear it may come crashing down
breaking us into pieces all over again

fragile
in all its stability

*I will help fix what's been broken*

Contemplating if my choice to simply look but keep walking is
        a mistake

If I take this last piece with me home

I can see it when I want

and enjoy it's comfort

Invest on its upkeep and do what's necessary
to make this gem last a lifetime

but why should I?

Why continue the same routine with a different expectation?

This gallery is familiar because I was trapped in it once

Hoping

      Wondering

              waiting

for you to want to step into my gallery

*I will show you my truth*

But what will you do with it?

Would you hang my piece in your gallery for all to see?

Keep it for your heart

that's all I wanted

See because I made it for us

Just for *our art*

For our portraits to hang beside one another

*strong*

*beautiful*
*complete*

like you.

Your portrait is perfect in all that you do

# Because

Waking up in night sweats,
     shadow by the door
Heart rate increases,
     can't take no more.

This a new introduction or ones from before? How can I be
  sure?
Panic by the floor.
Try to move around, make sound
someone has to hear.
Twisted with my demons
shit they whisper in my ear.

"No one cares little misfit, they'll never believe ..."

Manipulation sinks in as my throat tightening.

*Sting!*

Can I win?

Drifting out of sight.
Room spins, ripped innocence.
so why fight?
Every single try only led me to bleed.
Any way you call it rape,
      it affected me.
These types of things
      minds can't forget.
fuckin over and over

A broken cassette
is locked in the back
stored away in your mind.

When you face your reflection, flashed to the times
They made you watch
simple touch or a glare …

Teleports right back, no matter how prepared.

Or how many sessions of this damn therapy

I can still
 feel its touch

I can still
 see its teeth …

Dance within my misery
it rocks me to sleep

Used to lay by my side,
now it's placed underneath.

Anxiety,
Depression,
PTSD …


Survived the war                                        now it's time
     to breathe.


Please

don't take this lightly

I'm still in pain.
I still feel broken

I still feel shame.

shoulda fought harder
coulda broke free ...

Shoulda wrote the words
I was too scared to speak.

Now I feel weak, deep to the core.

smaller, growing, being
cries,
wait there'll be more

Pain into action, no matter how sore
cuz I felt that impact
so I'm locking that door

# Where the End begins

I tried to do my best, gave this my all
I confess ... I made some mistakes

I coulda turned away

but ya stomped on my heart
then asked why I'm not okay

Told me once before, in time you would change.
Flip the script blame my traits, don't know how
can't explain

When I think about your name
it brings tears
dripping pain

Never one to blame but you're the reason I'm this way.
Clearly couldn't see
Find a way to blame on me instead of saying sorry
broken track
break the cycle how 'bout that?

but it'll never come to play cuz you're angry at yourself
Honesty is hard to say.

Were angry, we're hurt, but this life ain't a curse,
Find a way to push it through and I will value all my worth.

Old habits laid to rest
Build a whole new family tree,
because our kids deserve the best.

Realization of abuse didn't start with me and you.

Traced back secrets of our truth

now faced what to do?

Time to deal with mental health, growing hole up in my chest
Reliving vivid memories wish I can get a fucking rest, damn!
It's playing in my mind

Jumping back to square one as I look into your eyes

trying to be better
it's getting hard to breathe …

went against my *own* beliefs and began some *therapy*
What did it teach?
There's so much more to do.
Ending broken family cycles, it begins with me and you.

Were angry, we're hurt, but this life ain't a curse,
Find a way to push it through and I will value all my worth.

Old habits laid to rest
Build a whole new family tree,
because our kids deserve the best.

# Virtue Development

Psychological development stages were brought together with
successful and unsuccessful outcomes after dealing with
crisis.

Birth-1year old's: the child learns a sense of trust/mistrust

1–3-year old's: Autonomy vs Shame & Doubt, develop
independence or doubt abilities.
Failure brings self-doubt/shame.

Staying up fighting sleep dreams make me weep, caught up in a
hustle can I set my mind free?
Staring at reflections not liking what I seen.
Next thing ya know he's grabbing me at the knees,

pulling off my tights,

then comes the skirt.

Nothing
in this life
can ever cover up the hurt.

Pain runs deep, so does the fears.
screaming in my head, covering my ears.

whispers to say, *it's gonna be alright*

Just another dark visit in the depths of the night
Try to put up a fight hands won't close

Clench a pillowcase cuz there's no more clothes
Scratching on the walls why can't they hear?

Continues to endure another ten years

Not just him, every one of my peers
family and friends don't believe the tears.

Fight or flight response had it up to here.
Tried to tell the story

message wasn't clear

Report for nothin' cops don't care, no evidence so no case there.
Can't understand.
They thought that I would.
Take me back to church think it makes it all good

Little do they know about the pastor too ... He preaches to the
    choir but abuses the youth.
Is there a lesson to learn or will God push through?
Raised up in a world shocked and confused.
Left and abused, cease to believe
a will to survive.

mind can't breathe

Like a disease, corruption of time.
Body looks healed, mind's in a bind.

First comes the crime then comes the doom
Speakers drown the sound call it hop hop boom
Bat beneath her feet heart skips a beat
Nightmares turned real after dark, as she sleeps.

Creeping down the halls flashin' more than memories.

Notebook full of rage, a world can't see.
Traumatized past buried underneath.
Years fly by, still can't see.

growing up teen, behind locked doors.

intimacy not desired for sure.

Men she came across failed to understand her love.
Diamond in the rough more like rocky road

Tears melt by, watching hearts explode
scraping out the bucket nothin left of hope

call it pain of neglect

Finally cut the rope …     times can't forget.

now cuz it all builds up
screaming out the tunnels left her stuck in a rut

Begins to cut, in attempt an escape …
Middle school kid tried to control the pain.

Now comes the change, then comes the truth.
Perception change overtime, vision for the youth.
If we never speak, we'll never really know.

So I cut my wounds open, let the world have a show.
Water more than seeds, let it all be known.
Strength after strain, takes time to grow … Believe in ya self
let the light show.

3–5-year old's: Initiative Vs. Guilt;
Self-control develops, *failure* brings anxiety,
guilt, feeling irresponsible

5–12-year old's: Industry Vs. Inferiority;
Academic and social world skills develop, comparing themselves
    to others
measuring success or failure.
When failed, kids feel incompetent and develop low self esteem

As the brain develops, we realize the circumstances
we've dealt with aren't always in our control.
What we can control is what we do next.
I choose to relive this, to provide vivid imagery
of what almost broke me to show what built me.
I hope it can do the same for you.

# Loving Reflection

The imperfections were a blessing.
Open my eyes so I can stand to see, you didn't take my heart
    away, no … I set it free.

These conversations with myself got me questioning the time, if
    I can take a day to take it back
would I still make you mine?

Say I'm hopeless but I'm focused yet your love has got me blind
Cross sided I'm misguided as I take another lie.
Say our words are more than golden, truth will slowly start
    unfolding.
Went from endless love to just mistrust.
Look at you felt disgust. Now I don't know if I trust myself to
    make a move.
Never meant to play the fool guess it's my turn now to lose.

Messages you hide from me …

Trust my gut, can't believe …

Days with her
Nights with me

Drying tears oh can't you see? Pain inflicted to my soul

Loving you I lost control.

Grasp a hold on what was left, said okay babe I do confess.
I love you but her I won't leave, fading sounds cannot breathe
We have a baby, what's this mean? How you say this shit to me?
Screamin' bangin' on ya chest …
Say you're sorry fuck the rest

Promises that you do neglect, happiness there is no more left.

Done with us you failed the test. No more love, only distress.

Leaving you was ugly but I finally feel refreshed.

Till a day you broke the mold, took you back take a toll.
Emotions turning cold
an empty vessel
loving soul.

Falling love, falling chances, used to be hopeless romantic.
Love and belonging came to me, now it feels like a bad dream.

Recognition of my strength, without change we can't embrace.
Realize beauty grows from pain              expressive words
      unlocking chains.

Brought me healing not revealing all the pressure caused to me.
Lying with apologies ...  Lovesick caused a tragedy.


My reflection showed neglection,
where happiness used to be.

Love is blind but now I see,
loving you was bad for me.

Cautious love lost in a daze
Guarded heart it's just my ways.
Companionship I didn't do,
love can leave an eternal bruise.

Told you that I was cool off this, puppy love can just feel like
      bliss ... One night that ended with a kiss ...
coulda saved myself from all of this ...

Shoulda stayed in my lane this I missed

Face what repercussion is, convinced me to give it a try.

To doubt myself
oh why would I,
stoop to less than what I'm worth?

Played me man you got some nerve

Turned to pages of our time,
 those love letters I made them fly ... back-to-back every holi-
    day

Broken memories fade astray.


Did you even really love me or was it something just to say?

Was it all a bluff cuz clearly what I gave was not enough. Now
    I'm growing and it's showing
no desire left to touch.

Falling love, falling chances, used to be hopeless romantic.
Love and belonging came to me, now it feels like a bad dream.

Recognition of my strength, without change we can't embrace.
Realize beauty grows from pain            expressive words
    unlocking chains.

Brought me healing not revealing all the pressure caused to me.
Lying with apologies ... Lovesick caused a tragedy.

My reflection showed neglection
where happiness used to be.
Love is blind but now I see, loving you was bad for me.

# Endless

Man ... tell em' bout the Bay
and tell em' bout our lives and the way we was raised.
Holding down what we got seems it's not okay. Every time I tell
    my story, reactions a long face. Don't be sorry for me cuz see
    it put me in a place, yeah I was scared and what not
Built through fear becomes grace

Warrior of peace
pain non existent

Shielded from the waste cuz change is persistent.
Don't let toxins get in quicksand covers all.
Once you take a step in, watch ya step never fall

Different world were livin' in, protect ya neck.

Watch you sink not swim, forgive don't forget.
Damage has been done, we face what's here ... Repercussions
    never come just a foggy shattered mirror.

Divine in the eyes
who holds the key?

Past the pupils through the mind dreams unfold beautifully.
Love in the eyes, refrain come next.

Blink of an eyelash now it's time to reflect.

Surround by peers, still I can't get through
opportunities for years ... break the walls push it through
Chains can't hold back from a dream's impact.

Tryna find a way to change let my lyrics do that.
Nobody hears the vision unless its mumble rap.
Not my cup of tea, prefer old school boom bat.

Hip hop is a mission we're all in route.
No chasing dreams or reason everybody chasing clout. To live
    without a world unheard. You are who you kick it with,
    never lost here's the word,
Remain humble, sun can always turn its weather.
Dark days return feeling stronger than ever.
Relax my mind unwind lost time,
shadow boxing lost thoughts,
tracing back lost rhymes

See I'm doing fine
if you ask me what I say?
Raised from the dirt, buried hope, and found a way. No you
    can't understand nightmares untold.

Place yo feet where we sleep, endless stories turn ya cold.
Unimaginable scenes
never seemed to get old.
Time after time, a cycle repeats this the end of our youth or can
    we stand to defeat?

Empty promises mean nothin'
Cormega wrote to speak.
Dropping knowledge and hope on every single beat. Old soul
    mentality taught me this not that. Wise minds come to-
    gether there's a melody for that.

Call it rhythm, rhymes, with a little bit of pain … Add some
    poetry in, a new art form remains.
Drag us up out the pit we've created in our brains.

Take a step back, inhale create a new plan

Nas spoke it to the kids believe I know that I can … be what
    I wanna be. Work day to day. Be all that I can be stronger
    bonds never fade.

Help ya people get up don't shoot find a way

Statistics say we got no goals ... Stop to understand how it
affects us as a whole.

If we all sit down and stomp our feet..
temper tantrums won't solve a gad damn thing.

Use ya voice to speak utilize ya rights.

If you got em, be grateful and do what's right. Stand for the
pushed down, take stand, take flight.
Soaring past finish lines they hoped we might ... Give up or
give in.
Bet we changed their minds.

A phase in time blind leads the blind, next thing we see
hate attacks and crime.

Shooting left to right, rising death rates.
New fate for these times or can we all escape? Last of dying
breed no time to wait.
An effort to build, an effort to change. Feed the minds of our
youth show 'em what to do.

Opportunities are endless
it all depends on you.

## Acknowledgements

This journey would not have been what it is without art and pain simultaneously dancing amongst one another in every day of life. The scars now reside where the hopelessness once lived, embracing unlocked potentials with every tear shared.

My Beauties ... Who watered my heart when it crumbled to dirt. Tenderly tended to my growth and always brought sunshine and laughs while being honest with the steps and at times the raw words I needed to hear to ensure I didn't let the world get the best of me. I knew you two wouldn't let that happen. Your words, I needed to hear to be who I am now. Without the chosen few family, my heart wouldn't be standing here today.

To my little big sister Prissilla, thank you for loving me so beautifully. I love our memories and hold them and your traits close to me always. Everything reminds me of you. You helped mold the pieces I call myself. You made me rap my heart out that night, and gave me what I needed to breathe ever since. I love you forever. I miss you every day. I'll always be your big little sissy. I miss you so much.

To my Best Friend and Sister Marissa. We made it this far bz imagining what else life has for us. Thank you for being my strength and not letting me give in. Every freestyle ever spit with you helped me speak another day into my world. From best friends to sisters, you melted your place in my heart forever. The harmony you create within music melts onto damaged souls and reminds me why I continue to thrive. You inspire me more every day with your glow and resilience to succeed in life's endeavors. You are hope. I love you forever hunny always.

To my Best Friend and Sister Ava, my heart in the form of a goddess too strong to be broken. All you've done within my heart cannot be measured with simple words. You're the speaker of my thoughts when I felt unheard, my best friend, and thankfully after an eternity of memories later, my sister in love that I'll never let go of. I love you always. Thank you for being the armor my heart needed and for loving me this much. You remind me why I need to be strong with the way you loved me. I've always admired the way you don't let anything keep you down; I'll cherish you always.

To my Best Friend Ginevra, you're always reminding me of how far I've come and I'd like to remind you how far your presence has also brought us. As you fill more of my memories with your welcoming support and care, I'm reminded why you're such a huge piece of my heart, You show love how to be loved. You've inspired me to try to open up more and be my true self, wounds and all. Thank you for never judging me for what I was already beating up myself about. Most importantly, for the courage you gave me.

And to the piece that picked up my fallen pieces, Luis. Thank you for being my rock. That night I fell into your arms crying endlessly, I knew my heart would be forever safe within yours. I promise to keep your love in the light it deserves to shine in. Love you to infinity and beyond Handsome.

And ... Mom,
I hope you made it to this part. I wish I could hug you forever. I'm sorry if it feels like I'm not trying. All I want is for your heart to receive what it deserves ... Endless love.
Thank you for trying. I know it wasn't easy.
You are love.

# Resources

**Childhelp National Child Abuse Hotline**
childhelphotline.org
(800) 422-4453

**Crisis Text Line**
crisistextline.org
Text HOME to 741741

**Nacional de Prevención del Suicidio**
suicidepreventionlifeline.org/help-yourself/en-espanol/
(888) 628-9454

**National Domestic Violence Hotline**
thehotline.org
(800) 799-7233

**National Sexual Assault Hotline**
rainn.org
(800) 656-4673

**National Suicide Prevention Lifeline**
suicidepreventionlifeline.org
(800) 273-8255

*For TTY/Deaf or Hard of Hearing Users*:
suicidepreventionlifeline.org/help-yourself/for-deaf-hard-of-hearing/
Use your preferred relay service or dial 711 then 1-800-273-8255

**Substance Abuse and Mental Health Services Administration National Helpline**
samhsa.gov/find-help/national-helpline
(800) 662-4357

## About the Author

In Lisa's words:

This collection is to provide insight and awareness to the hushed topics all too familiar that many endure daily. I dive into pathways of damaged roads traveled and unlock along the way ... I reflect on family secrecy, sexual abuse, infertility, physical/internal trauma, healing, police brutality, addiction, love, breaking barriers, and social issues. My goal is to shine a light on these difficult topics in hopes that it reveals what can be changed for a better outcome internally and overall. I do this by sharing vividly my truth, thoughts, self reflections and embracing that this vulnerability can be what molds a new cycle of healing.

Sisneroz is a student at Mission College in Santa Clara, California where she is majoring in Psychology.

## About the Press

Thera Books is an independent publishing house based in Sacramento, California. We aim to publish writers pushing the boundaries of literature and writing about what it means to be human.

www.thetherabooks.com

A SPACE FOR YOU TO WRITE ... WHAT'S YOUR STORY?

A SPACE FOR YOU TO WRITE ... WHAT'S YOUR STORY?

A SPACE FOR YOU TO WRITE ... WHAT'S YOUR STORY?

www.ingramcontent.com/pod-product-compliance
Lightning Source LLC
Chambersburg PA
CBHW030459130626
46549CB00007B/2790